At Odds With God

Adult Bible Study
And Sermon Resource

Peter C. Garrison

CSS Publishing Company, Inc.
Lima, Ohio

AT ODDS WITH GOD

Scripture quotations are from the *New Revised Standard Version of the Bible,*
copyright 1989 by the Division of Christian Education of the National Council of
the Churches of Christ in the USA. Used by permission.

Library of Congress Cataloging-in-Publication Data

Garrison, Peter C., 1951-
 At odds with God : the problems between God's will and us his people / by Peter
C. Garrison.
   p.   cm.
 ISBN 1-55673-520-0
 1. God—Will—Meditations. 2. Spiritual life—Christianity. 3. Worship programs.
I. Title.
BV4501.2.G368   1993
248.4—dc20   93-29491
                                                                        CIP

ISBN 1-55673-520-0
PRINTED IN U.S.A.

*To Joanne, my wife,
and John, my son.*

Acknowledgments

Thank you to Mr. Bill Marshall for his "hit and run" editing of my manuscript. You can come out now, Bill — I'm not mad anymore ...

Oh God my Father, I am seeking You,
not making statements about You.
Help me and guide me.

— St. Augustine "Confessions" 9, 17

Table Of Contents

Purpose Of This Book   7

How To Use This Book   9

Chapter 1   11
Adam And Eve, The First People
Questions About The Story
Reflections
A Prayer Starter
Suggestions For Practicing Your Prayer
Suggested Order Of Worship

Chapter 2   19
Balaam, The Donkey And The Angel
Questions About The Story
Reflections
A Prayer Starter
Suggestions For Practicing Your Prayer
Suggested Order Of Worship

Chapter 3   29
King Ahaz, Idolater
Questions About The Story
Reflections
A Prayer Starter
Suggestions For Practicing Your Prayer
Suggested Order Of Worship

Chapter 4   41
Pontius Pilate, Pragmatic
Questions About The Story
Reflections
A Prayer Starter
Suggestions For Practicing Your Prayer
Suggested Order Of Worship

Chapter 5   51
    Judas, The Obscure
    Questions About The Story
    Reflections
    A Prayer Starter
    Suggestions For Practicing Your Prayer
    Suggested Order Of Worship

Chapter 6   59
    Ananias And Sapphira, Liars
    Questions About The Story
    Reflections
    A Prayer Starter
    Suggestions For Practicing Your Prayer
    Suggested Order Of Worship

The Purpose Of This Book

The purpose of this book is to help your will find delight in the will of God.

You might not think this is much of a challenge, but then, that's precisely the problem. As St. Augustine puts it, *Non posse non peccare* — "We are not able not to sin," and our original sin is our will opposing God's. This conflict may keep us from living a life full of joy now and forever.

Through the drama of these speculations and playlets, you are confronted with the reality of the conflict between good and evil, right and wrong, morality and immorality.

Through the study of scripture that this book promotes, you will see that God's will for you is merciful, just, patient, slow to anger and abounding in steadfast love. It is his will that we live forever with him. He sent his Son Jesus to show us this will and make us sure of his love for us. He sends his Holy Spirit to move our will to his: To love him and to love our neighbor. His will be done!

How To Use This Book

This book can be used as a pulpit resource for sermons during Lent, adult Bible study or individual reflection.

Each "Conflict Of The Will" is put into a speculative biblical setting that is refreshing to the reader. The conflict is put in contemporary terms and is expressed in a short story, dramatic soliloquy or a playlet for two or three readers. (Both the short story and the soliloquy can be read in parts if you wish.)

Following the conflict are "Questions About The Story/ Questions For You." These questions lead you to recognize the conflict as your own and not as theoretical as they seemed at first.

In each chapter, a "Reflection By A Famous Christian" shares an example of how your will can find delight in God's will. Finally, "A Prayer Starter" welcomes you to turn your will to God's in prayer and action. Finally, "Suggestions For Practicing Your Prayers" helps you to live the life you ask for in God's will.

Included at the end of each chapter is a "Suggested Order For Worship." This 45-minute setting includes the "conflict," prayers, small-group discussion, and suggested hymns.

chapter one

Adam And Eve, The First People

Eve envies God's wisdom. Adam doesn't take God's word of warning as real. Basically, these people's problem is that they always want to be first, even before God. If you don't think this is a problem, then that's a problem. It's called "Original Sin."

(Please read Genesis, Chapter 3)

Adam And Eve

Adam was first. There is a certain comfort in being second or third, next or last, in the middle or part of a crowd: One can hide or ask for help or consider alternatives or grow impatient or slink away unnoticed. But Adam enjoyed no such luxuries. Adam was first and if anything was going to get done, such as tilling the ground, Adam had to do it.

Adam's problem was that he got used to being first. After a while, Adam would allow nothing to be first before him. He'd get up before the sun arose. "I'm up already," he'd shout to the startled birds. He was the first to explore paradise and try out things first such as smelling a new flower or wading through a secluded pond.

One day, Eve came along.

Eve was, of course, second. Adam reminded her of this often. "I'm first," he'd sniff and stride off towards some elysian goal. "Follow me," he'd say, "Follow me," butting into Eve's afternoon stroll. Eve had her pride, too. She would sigh and go off another direction completely.

Today she'd come to a stop leaning on a sign Adam had put up next to a berry bush that was ready to be picked. The sign said, "First dibs." Eve sat alone wondering what good she was if Adam didn't need her to do anything but follow him around.

After all, she was made to be with Adam: A "helper as his partner," God had put it. Of course, "Helper" didn't mean an assistant or servant. It meant someone who was, "equal, different and suitable."

She felt equal. She certainly felt different than Adam. But as for suitable, Adam didn't share much of himself except his back as he rushed off to be first at something or other.

Eve sighed a short shallow sigh. A curious blackbird jumped over to her and cocked his head sideways to cast a yellow eye up to her. Uncharacteristically pouty, she gave it a dainty kick into a thicket. The blackbird scolded her in that throaty way blackbirds have. It flew off over paradise toward the east.

Eve's eyes followed the blackbird and her gaze settled on something at which Adam had not yet had a chance to be first: THE TREE.

It was a lovely tree. God had named it the tree "of the knowledge of good and evil." The only reason Adam had not been first to eat of its fruit is that God himself had gotten first dibs on it. "You may freely eat of every tree of the garden; but of the tree of the knowledge of good and evil you shall not eat, for in the day that you eat of it you shall die."

This prohibition from God only called Adam's attention all the more to the tree. Who did God think he was anyway? Adam so wanted to be first at everything. Now God had put this beautiful tree here in the middle of the garden and Adam couldn't even be second. (As if that really counted . . .)

Eve could see Adam over by a stream. She suspected he was again fussing about this constraint on his freedom. He'd mumble and skip a stone, pace back and forth along the bank and toss in a bigger rock with a "plunk," sit down and twiddle with his toes.

Eve felt sorry for Adam. She did want to help him, that was her calling in life; to help him as an equal, in a suitable way, perhaps some way that was different. She thought about how she could help him and was so absorbed in this that when the serpent coiled up next to her it was such a surprise that she let out a little shriek. "Oh," she said. "Don't sneak up on me like that."

The crafty serpent didn't say he was sorry. He had too much on his crafty little serpent mind. He knew how Eve could help Adam in a very different way. The serpent asked, "Did God say, 'You shall not eat from any tree in the garden'?"

Eve thought a moment. No, that wasn't the prohibition. God wasn't so strict as to prohibit eating from any tree, just the one. Life wasn't so prohibitive after all. Why did the serpent misquote God?

13

"No," Eve replied. "We may eat of the fruit of the trees in the garden." She went on to explain the one constraint God had put on Adam and herself; the one that frustrated Adam's "me first" compulsion. "You shall not eat of the fruit of the tree that is in the middle of the garden, nor shall you touch it, or you shall die."

But, thinking back on God's exact words, Eve realized she too had just now misquoted him. God didn't say that they couldn't even touch the fruit; Eve had made that up. "Maybe," she thought to herself, "maybe I am a little perturbed myself with this one silly restriction. After all, we are God's image. What's the deal? Doesn't God trust us? Who does he think he is?"

Then the serpent said an amazing thing with the next sentence he spoke. Years later, long years of fear and pain later, Eve would look back on this moment and wonder why, when the serpent spoke, the world did not crack and shatter and fall about her and the serpent like sharp stones.

The serpent told Eve that God was a liar.

He put it this way: "You will not die; for God knows that when you eat of it your eyes will be opened, and you will be like God knowing good and evil."

Eve gasped. The warm breeze made her shiver. Her mind raced, "What a thing to say about God! Who does this serpent think he is, God almighty? Oh, what a thing for him to say."

But as Eve looked at the beautiful tree that delighted her eyes, and saw the good fruit hanging on the branches, the tree seemed to hold the answers to her worries — it would make her wise and she would think like God and know just what to do for Adam and for herself.

Before she knew it, her mouth was full of fruit. She noted she was not dead. She took more bites and she mumbled through the delicious fruit, "Who does he think he is, anyway?"

Questions About The Story
Questions For You

(This story is fictional, based on the scripture quotations found in it. However, the basic conflict between God's will and the will of humanity is not fictional. The following questions based on this conflict may help you see that your conflict with God is real because: You're real and God is real.)

1. Why is having to be first a problem for Adam?
2. Is being first a problem for you? Name two ways it is a problem.
3. Who is really "first" in your life?
4. When Eve asks, "Who does he think he is, anyway?" is she asking about God, Adam or the serpent? Could she ask this of herself?
5. Why does everyone but the serpent ask this question in the story? Does he know who God thinks he is?
6. Do you ever question God's authority in your life? How?
7. Do you ask God who he is, too? What does he answer?
8. Do you ever ask God who you are? What do you hear?
9. "Original sin" is not being content with being the image of God, but wanting instead to be God. How does this "wanting to be first" hurt people today? Creation? Ourselves? Our church? Our nation? Our economy?
10. How is Eve's being helpful really being harmful?
11. When you carefully examine Eve's motives, who is she really helping?
12. Read Genesis 3 again. What do you think is the root of original sin?
13. How do Adam and Eve react to God when he confronts them with their sin? (Genesis 3:8-13) Why is this reaction another aspect of "pride," "me first-ness," or "original sin?"
14. If we are still in sin, how do we know God loves us?

Reflection By A Famous Christian On:
Original Sin

"I know, of course, what bad consciences do when they begin to make themselves aprons from fig leaves to try and hide themselves. (Genesis 3:7) Since they misinterpret God's Word and follow their own fancy, it is easy also to judge their heart by the scriptures, which teach us that the wicked have no rest: 'His heart is like a wave of the sea, which cannot rest.' " (Isaiah 57:20)

— Martin Luther — *Luther's Works*, Vol. 37, page 29, Fortress Press 1961. Edited by Robert H. Fischer.

A Prayer Starter

Lord, give me a simple faith to trust the simple Word of God. Help me to hear his love clearly in Christ and to share it simply through the gentle guidance of the Holy Spirit. Help me to know when I am hiding from the truth, from God and from myself. Help me to put God first, the truth first, and myself first only in service to others to the glory of God.

Suggestions For Practicing Your Prayer

1. What words of Christ give me the most comfort? Read or recite them outloud now.
2. How can the Holy Spirit guide me in this comfort today?
3. How can I share this comfort with someone today?
4. What other ways can I resist the urge to always put my will first? (Practice saying, "After you," to people you meet. For example, let them go first through doorways, into buses, elevators and grocery market check-out lines.)

A Suggested Order Of Worship For Adam And Eve, The First People

(Note: You may want to break into small groups for discussion of the story and then join together again for the closing worship. If so, select discussion leaders to help people reflect on the questions in the book. Or, you may want to stay together and reflect silently as the questions are read.)

Opening: Greeting and introduction of "The Conflict Of The Will: Our Envy Of Our All-Knowing God."

Hymns: "He Leadeth Me" or "Immortal, Invisible, God Only Wise"

Read: Introduction to Chapter One, page 11

Meditation: Adam And Eve, The First People

Discussion: Break into discussion groups and follow "Questions About The Story/Questions For You" or read aloud for group silent reflection. When finished, quietly return to worship setting.

Read: "Reflections By A Famous Christian"

Read: "Prayer Starter"

Invitation: Invite people to add their own prayers

Read: "Suggestions For Practicing Your Prayer"

The Lord's Prayer

The Apostles' Creed

Hymns: "How Great Thou Art" or "Now Thank We All Our God"

Benediction And Dismissal: "Go in peace and serve the Lord."

chapter two

Balaam,
The Donkey
And The Angel

At first glance, Balaam, the donkey and the angel don't have a problem. They tried to do exactly what God wanted them to do. But God seemed to change his mind about what he wanted Balaam to do for him. The following fiction is about how Balaam, the donkey and the angel puzzle out God's apparent change of mind. Have you ever tried to figure out God?

(This chapter finds its "confusion" in the uncertainty of one ancient Hebrew word concerning the motivation of the angel of the Lord, in Numbers 22:32b.)

(Please read Numbers 22)

Balaam, The Donkey
And The Angel

Balaam, the Donkey and the Angel sit together in a narrow path between some vineyards. Balaam is still puzzled that his donkey can talk. The presence of the angel still makes him nervous, but an angel-of-the-Lord is an angel-of-the-Lord and what can you do? Balaam decides to review some of the events leading up to this embarrassing situation of his misunderstanding a donkey, an angel and God. Was he supposed to go to the foreign King Balak or not? Was he supposed to curse God's people or not? Was the angel there to scare him, warn him or give him this talkative donkey who won't be quiet now that he's got the gift of gab?

Balaam: Okay, Okay . . . I didn't set out to get confused here. As far as I can remember, it seems to me God changed his mind about me going to curse his people on behalf of this foreign king named Balak, son of Zippor of Moab. Weird names . . .

Angel: *(Piously)* How could you get confused about God? He would never allow you to go and curse his people. As an angel, which, by the way, means "messenger," I would never doubt God's intention for his people's good. I would do what he says and get on with it. Does it seem to you that God changes his mind, so what? He's God.

Balaam: Well, aren't you a goodie-two-shoes. No wonder you're an angel . . .

Angel: *(Hotly)* Okay, smart guy. Let's review how you goofed up.

Donkey: I'll tell you how he goofed up. He hit me. Not once; but three times!

Balaam: Don't start braying about that again. I apologize. I didn't see the angel. I didn't know why you veered off the road into a field, smacked into a wall and then collapsed. My "anger was kindled," I just got mad at you. I had enough to do trying to figure out God: God changing his mind on me: "Go to Balak. Don't go to Balak. Go."

Donkey: So, God can't change his instruction to you? His plans didn't fit your sense of order, so you hit me? Am I not your donkey, which you have ridden all your life to this day? I only veered, smacked and collapsed because I saw this angel with a sword in his hand standing in front of us. Don't you think that's a good enough reason to "veer" once in my life?

Balaam: I said I was sorry and I meant it.

Angel: Me too, Donkey. I didn't mean to scare you. God's anger was kindled because [Balaam] was going . . . I took my stand in the road.

Balaam: But that's what bothers me when I look back on the whole thing: First God told me, "You shall not go with them; you shall not curse my people for they are blessed." That made sense; the Israelites are God's own people, why mess with them? I told Balak's guys to forget it. But more officials show up, I resist them and say, ". . . I could not go beyond the command of the Lord my God, to do less or more."

Angel: But you knew God might have more to say to you.

Balaam: Yes, but he seemed to change his mind completely and told me to, ". . . get up and go with them; but do only what I tell you to do."

Donkey: So, what's the matter? Trust God, Balaam.

Balaam: I trust God, I do — really. I take on his change of plans, and then an angel with a sword shows up and my donkey goes out of control. I got so mad!

Donkey: I know! You threatened to kill me. You were so upset at seeing a fool, that it didn't startle you a bit that your donkey was talking.

Balaam: Listen, lately I've been talking with God . . . anything is possible.

Angel: *(Piously)* But have you been *listening* to God?

Balaam: *(Aside to Donkey)* Angels can be irritating, you know that?

Donkey: Tell me about it. He scared the hell out of me.

Angel: You're getting pretty familiar. You weren't so casual when the Lord opened your eyes and you saw me standing in the road with my drawn sword. You fell on your face. It's a good thing too. Had you kept coming, I would have killed you and let the donkey live.

Balaam: Okay, okay, I messed up with the donkey. But how was I supposed to know that God was trying to tell me not to go to Balak? I admit, "I have sinned, for I did not know that you were standing in the road to oppose me. Now, therefore, if it is displeasing to you, I will return home." From now on, I just want some plain explicit instructions about what God is going to want from me.

Angel: What's your point, exactly?

Balaam: *(Exasperated)* Oooh. The point is that it's unfair that God seems to change his mind and doesn't let me know about it. I don't understand his plans and then I look like a fool with this donkey, and then you almost end up killing me. It seems unfair, unkind, embarrassing . . .

Angel: And my angelic point is that only God is in control. Get used to it. The reason I blocked your way was because it was "perverse" before me. *(Numbers 22:32b. The Ancient Hebrew word thought to be "perverse" is obscure and not known for sure.)*

Balaam: My way was what before you? I didn't hear you.

Angel: Actually, it doesn't matter why I did what I was sent to do. What matters is that God commanded it to be done. Shall I pose an allegory concerning God and you; you and your donkey?

Balaam: A what?

Donkey: A connecting story between how you reacted to me and how you react to God.

Balaam: Smart donkey. Okay, fine. But I better not end up being God's donkey.

Angel: Listen. Think how you reacted to the donkey doing his best to avoid what he recognized as a danger.

Donkey: Yeah. You hit me. Big man.

Balaam: Well, I didn't know what you were doing. I thought that after all these years, you'd gone nuts. I wondered if I could trust you. I forgot you were my friend. We'd been everywhere together.

Angel: Do you see any connection yet between your not trusting your donkey and your not trusting God?

Balaam: What? You mean my not trusting God after all this time? Yeah. I see what you're getting at . . . I got mad instead of trusting my life-long donkey. Now I'm mad at my life-long God. I should trust God even when it seems he's nuts.

Angel: I wouldn't put it that way ...

Balaam: No, you wouldn't. But I get your point. God is in control and God loves his people, he loves me. I'm sorry I got so angry.

Donkey: Make sure it doesn't happen again.

Angel: Yeah, watch your reaction to problems. God is with you.

Donkey: Somehow you'd goofed up and God was setting you on the right path again. That's no reason to get mad at me or wonder about God's goodness.

Balaam: Yeah, you're right. I just wish God would tell me what I should do.

Donkey: I wonder what's down the road for us.

Angel: I just happen to know.

Balaam: Tell me!

Angel: Balaam, you're doing it again. Trust God.

Balaam: I knew you'd say that.

Questions About The Story
Questions For You

(The playlet is fictional, based on the scripture quotations found in it. However, the basic conflict of being puzzled and frustrated at God's will is not fictional. You will be asked questions based on this conflict and see your conflict with God as real because: You're real and God is real.)

1. God seems to change his mind in Numbers 22, verse 20. Do you see this as a problem? Does Balaam?
2. When does Balaam get angry at the way things are going? Could this have anything to do with Balaam's frustration with being God's servant? (v. 27)
3. Is Balaam a faithful servant of God?
4. How does God, the angel of the Lord and the donkey help Balaam to be a faithful servant? (vv. 24, 33)
5. When did you last ask God, "Hey, what's going on here?"
6. Who helps you to be a faithful servant? Family? Friends? Prayer? The Sacraments? Church? Pastor? Confession?
7. Do you ask God what's going on during really good times?
8. What do you think God is "up to" in your life right now?
9. Who can help you to figure this out?
10. Is it necessary to "figure this out?"

Reflection By A Famous Christian On:
Puzzling Out God

This is a legend about St. Augustine: Augustine took a break from his writing one afternoon. He was writing about the trinity; about how God was one God in three persons.

As this is a mystery that is impossible for mortals to completely comprehend, Augustine was confused and frustrated. Off he went down the beach.

There was a little boy taking water from the Mediterranean Sea and pouring it from a bucket into a little hole he'd dug in the sand. Augustine asked the boy, "What are you doing?" The boy replied that he was attempting to put all the sea into this hole of his. "Stupid boy," Augustine observed.

The boy replied, "Not as stupid as you trying to explain God."

A Prayer Starter

Dear God, you are my God. I am your child. Help me to trust you and your love for me. You show your love for me plainly in the life, death and resurrection of Jesus. Help my soul to cling to you and for your right hand to sustain me.

Suggestions For Practicing Your Prayer

1. As you trust God today, what can you do to show this trust?

2. As you trust God today, what can you refrain from doing to show this trust?

3. Pray the *Our Father* three times a day this week. Take time to repeat three times each prayer: "... your will be done, on earth as in heaven ..."

A Suggested Order Of Worship
For
Balaam, The Donkey
And The Angel

(Note: You may want to break into small groups for discussion of the story and then join together again for the closing worship. If so, select discussion leaders to help people reflect on the questions in the book. Or, you may want to stay together and reflect silently as the questions are read.)

Opening: Greeting and introduction of "The Conflict Of The Will: Our Puzzlement At God's Perfect Will."

Hymns: "A Mighty Fortress Is Our God" or "Lord, Keep Us Steadfast In Your Word"

Read: Introduction to Chapter Two, page 19

Reading: Numbers 22

Meditation: Balaam, The Donkey And The Angel

Discussion: Break into discussion groups and follow "Questions About The Story/Questions For You" or read aloud for group silent reflection. When finished, quietly return to worship setting.

Read: "Reflections By A Famous Christian"

Read: "Prayer Starter"

Invitation: Invite people to add their own prayers

Read: "Suggestions For Practicing Your Prayer"

The Lord's Prayer

The Apostles' Creed

Hymns: "I Wonder As I Wander" or "Love Divine All Loves Excelling"

Benediction And Dismissal: "Go in peace and serve the Lord."

chapter three

King Ahaz, Idolater

King Ahaz has a real problem: he's worshiped about everything but the one true God; a blunder of cosmic proportions as we shall see. Could you be making the same mistake?

(Please read 2 Chronicles 28)

King Ahaz

King Ahaz sits outside heaven with a few other people. They are all waiting for something to happen or for someone to come and tell them something.

King Ahaz stands up. He walks back and forth. He clasps his hands together and unclasps them. He peers over the shoulders of the others who wait. Finally, he taps one person on the shoulder and asks:

Ahaz: What in the world are we standing around for?

Other: I don't know. I just got here.

Ahaz: Where did you come from?

Other: From dying.

Ahaz: Me too. *(Looks around)* No one seems too surprised by this situation. You'd think we'd be more surprised by life after death.

Other: It's no surprise. I think we all really knew there'd be life after death. We just didn't act like it while we were alive. Thinking about life after death can be scarier than thinking about just plain death. Anyway, the afterlife is pretty boring so far.

Ahaz: So, what happens now?

Other: So far this is it. Just standing or sitting and waiting.

Ahaz: Waiting for what? For whom?

Other: I don't know about you, but I'm tired of waiting. I'm going to look around. *(Starts to walk away ...)*

Ahaz: Wait. Don't leave. What are you looking for?

Other: A sign.

Ahaz: A sign? You mean like, WELCOME, or IN CASE OF AN EMERGENCY, or DANGER?

Other: No, a sign like an omen or clue about what's going on around here.

Ahaz: Do you believe in that omen stuff? I do.

Other: So do I. What kind of stuff do you believe in?

Ahaz: Well, first of all I don't believe in this "one God" thing. I can't see how one god can handle all of the world's concerns. It seems to me better to have a bunch of gods running around to take care of the local details. That way, each place gets its own god and each bunch of people their own protector. You know who to pay off.

Other: That sounds pretty handy. Also, it keeps the gods in line.

Ahaz: What do you mean?

Other: Well, what good is a god without worshipers to be a god of, or a place to be god at? If your god doesn't keep up the good work, then you can move to a different place or take up someone else's god. It keeps gods humble — in their place, if you get my meaning . . .

Ahaz: Yes. None of this, "You shall have no other gods before me," stuff. When I was king . . .

Other: Oh, you're a king?

31

Ahaz: Was . . . anyway, when I was a king, I worshiped about anything around. I hedged my bets . . . Who knows who's really in charge anyway? I cast images of Ba'als, I made offerings in Hinnom, I sacrificed my sons in fire, I left offerings on the high places, on the hills, and under every green tree. I was throwing offerings to gods the way some people throw bread crumbs to birds.

Other: That sounds a lot like the people I know. They depend on crystals, rabbits' feet, horse shoes, palm reading, horoscopes — lots of things . . .

Ahaz: Who divined your horoscopes for you?

Other: Divined? We read them in newspapers.

Ahaz: What's a newspaper?

Other: Wait a minute. You don't know what a newspaper is? Where have you been?

Ahaz: In Judah, Damascus, Israel and here, wherever "here" is.

Other: Something's not clear. When did you live?

Ahaz: My father Jothan died and I reigned after him for, let's see, 16 years. Then my son Hezekiah must have succeeded me. But, what's a newspaper?

Other: Oh my . . . You must have died thousands of years before me. I died in 199__. But we're both here now.

Ahaz: So, what's a newspaper?

Other: Will you stop asking me that? Don't you see what's happened? We both have been busy worshiping every thing and every god but the right one. I bet that's why we're just waiting around doing nothing; just waiting for nothing at all.

Ahaz: Uh-oh. I've heard of this place. We're "shades" of our former selves. Just bland existence from now on, forever. No ups and downs — just boredom. That's what some folks figured death might be like without God . . .

Other: What about an eternal life of peace and joy with your one God of Israel?

Ahaz: An academic question at this point, I guess. Especially for me. When I got stressed out being king, I grew even more faithless to the Lord.

Other: What did you do? *(Moving a little way off)* Maybe I ought not to be talking with you.

Ahaz: I'm ashamed to say.

Other: How could you make it any worse than it is now?

Ahaz: Well, I sacrificed to the gods of Damascus because Damascus had defeated me; I figured, "If you can't beat 'em, join 'em."

Other: I did that too in a way. I became so "scientific" and "critical" that I forgot to wonder. I believed the newspaper more than I did my own eyes. I believed the tabloids and ignored God's Word.

Ahaz: What's a tabloid . . .

Other: Don't change the subject. What else did you do to end up here?

Ahaz: I gathered together the utensils of the house of God, and cut them in pieces. I shut the doors of the temple and put up altars all over Jerusalem. Then I made high places for offerings to other gods. I ignored the Lord, the God of my ancestors.

Other: Well, maybe that's why we're just standing around. We ignored God or wanted him to leave us alone and so he has. He loved us and gave us what we really wanted: For God to leave us alone.

Ahaz: But it's so boring. Just waiting. One moment is just like the next. In fact, I'm not sure I recognize the idea of "next" anymore. One moment is just like another. One boring moment lasting forever. This doesn't seem like the way our loving Lord would treat us.

Other: Oh? He gives now what we wanted all through life: independence, leisure, no hassles, no "God above all gods" imposing his will on us by giving people those commandments.

Ahaz: Yeah, "Thou shall have no other Gods before me ..." He sounds jealous. I didn't like the limits he put on me.

Other: Obviously. But you forget one thing that came before any of the commandments: the promise of God. He always gives before he commands — he always loves first ... I read that somewhere.

Ahaz: What promise does he give us before those 10 commandments?"

Other: "I am the Lord your God ...," he said. He promises to be our God and for us to be his people.

Ahaz: Oh yeah. Oops.

Other: Oops is right. Oops forever, I guess. Neither one of us worshiped the one true God. We were once free to be with God but now we're trapped here away from God.

Ahaz: Nice irony, huh? He brought his people out of the house of slavery and we've stumbled right back into slavery again.

But, I suppose that's how we felt secure — as slaves; slaves to superstition, good luck, the petty whims of local gods who can be bribed, palm readers who would tell us what we wanted to hear, horoscopes telling us the cosmos made sense in a way that pleased our sense of order ...

Other: So, now what?

Ahaz: So, now *this* I guess.

Other: Our whole existence boils down to an eternity of, "I guess?"

Ahaz: I guess. I once had the certainty of the one true God and I lost it to the chancy nature of other gods. Where are they now?

Other: I once had certainty too. I thought good luck, the stars and planets or fortune cookies would help — four-leaf clovers, crossing my fingers ...

Ahaz: You were as nervous about life as I was. Why didn't we just trust our one true God who gave us life?

Other: Don't rub it in. I wish I would have known better. I guess I really did know better.

Ahaz: God knew us better. He gave us just what we wished for — time without him.

Other: Time forever, I guess. *(Sighs)*

Ahaz: *(Sighs)* I guess.

(Ahaz and the other turn back toward the expectant group of people who wait for someone, something.)

Questions About The Story
Questions For You

(The playlet is fictional, based on 2 Chronicles 28 and a mixture of ancient Mid-Eastern understandings of gods and life after death. However, the basic conflict between God's will and your will is not fictional. You will be asked questions based on this conflict and see your conflict with God as real because: You're real and God is real.)

1. Count the number of ways that King Ahaz worshiped other gods than the God of his ancestors, the one true God.
2. What was Ahaz's main motivation in worshiping the gods of his enemies?
3. What do you do in your life that may pay allegiance to something other than your living and jealous God?
4. What is your main motivation in this?
5. What do you think eternity will be like?
6. What do you think eternity will be like for those who do not believe in God?
7. Do you believe in God?
8. Why do you believe in God?

Reflection By A Famous Christian On:
Devotion To God Alone

"God, you made us for yourself and our souls are restless until they rest in thee."

— St. Augustine

A Prayer Starter

Dear Lord God, help me know you through Jesus, and to know myself as your dear child. Help me to worship only you and serve you with all my self. Help me to give my "self" to others for your glory.

Suggestions For Practicing Your Prayer

1. How did Jesus give himself to you and others? Why did he do this? (Hint: Read Matthew 36:29, John 3:16)

2. The Holy Spirit is God. How does the Holy Spirit share God's glory with you? (Hint: Read John 14:25-27)

3. God the Father is God. How does he "mother" you?

4. How can you, as an image of God, share God's love with another?

5. What is God's will for you?

6. How can you make sure this is God's will for you and not some personal whim of your own?

A Suggested Order Of Worship
For
King Ahaz, Idolater

(Note: You may want to break into small groups for discussion of the story and then join together again for the closing worship. If so, select discussion leaders to help people reflect on the questions in the book. Or, you may want to stay together and reflect silently as the questions are read.)

Opening: Greeting and introduction of "The Conflict Of The Will: Our Worshiping Something Or Someone Other Than The One True God."

Hymns: "Joyful, Joyful, We Adore Thee" or "Praise God From Whom All Blessings Flow"

Read: Introduction to Chapter Three, page 29

Reading: 2 Chronicles 28

Meditation: King Ahaz, Idolater

Discussion: Break into discussion groups and follow "Questions About The Story/Questions For You" or read aloud for group silent reflection. When finished, quietly return to worship setting.

Read: "Reflections By A Famous Christian"

Read: "Prayer Starter"

Invitation: Invite people to add their own prayers

Read: "Suggestions For Practicing Your Prayer"

The Lord's Prayer

The Apostles' Creed

Hymns: "Lord Of All Hopefulness" or "Savior Like A Shepherd Lead Us"

Benediction And Dismissal: "Go in peace and serve the Lord."

chapter four

Pontius Pilate, Pragmatic

Pontius Pilate's problem is that he is so practical, so cold-blooded, that he can ask, "What is truth," and never see it standing right before his eyes.

**(Please read Luke 13:1-5; Mark 15:1-15;
John 18:28—19:16; 1 Timothy 6:13)**

Pontius Pilate

The historian Josephus records that Pilate was replaced as Procurator of Judea for having executed Samaritan leaders who sought sacred vessels supposedly stored on Mount Gerizim since the days of Moses. Complaint was made to the Roman legate, Vitellius, and Pilate was sent in shame to Rome.

Christian tradition has it that Paul was imprisoned and later martyred in Rome. The setting for this dialogue supposes that Paul and Pilate meet in a Roman prison cell.

Paul: Let me ask the traditional prison question: What are you "in" for?

Pontius: As I see it, I am "in for" considerable trouble with my superiors. They judged me wrongly. All I did was persecute the leaders of a Samaritan revolt. Now I am sent back from Judea, and sit here in shame like you.

Paul: I, like you, was in trouble with my superior. However, unlike you, I am not ashamed. You see, my superior judged me rightly not wrongly. I had been persecuting him and he "corrected" me. He reprimanded me by striking me from my donkey and temporarily blinding me. I have since served him and now I am sent here, not in shame for me, but in glory to him.

Pontius: My superiors are the Roman Imperial Army and my emperor. I served them, and now their glory sends me shamefully here. Who is the superior you serve so bravely?

Paul: God. Jesus of Nazareth.

Pontius: Good God! I met him once. That Jesus! He once stood right before me: "Ecce homo; behold the man," I said.

Paul: Oh, he was more than mere man even then. However, I never saw him in the flesh. I only heard his voice and saw the bright light. Instead of my seeing the man he was, he saw me as the man I am — a sinner, who trusted my own goodness while doubting God's: a persecutor of God the king.

Pontius: I asked him if he were the King of the Jews.

Paul: What did he say?

Pontius: He told me I'd said so. Tricky answer.

Paul: I don't think he is so tricky as he is honest. I've found that his honesty makes you honest enough to tell the truth about yourself and about him. Now that can be "tricky;" to tell that truth.

Pontius: Then I'll ask you what I asked him — "What is truth?"

Paul: That's the wrong way to ask the question ...

Pontius: What do you mean? How else would you find the truth?

Paul: I don't think it's appropriate to ask "what" is truth, when "who" is truth asks the question more fully.

Pontius: Who? Jesus is the truth?

Paul: Yes. Think back. What did Jesus say exactly that made you ask your question concerning truth?

Pontius: I couldn't forget that. He said, "You say that I am a king. For this I was born, and for this I came into the world to testify to the truth. Everyone who belongs to the truth listens to my voice."

Paul: So, listen to him. Jesus is the truth as you listen to his voice; truth personified. Truth no longer a mere intellectual premise — but a personal relationship. Think of the depth of one's commitment to people, not a premise. You can never "belong" to some bloodless virtue called "truth." But you can belong to someone who is "true" and is "truth" himself. After all, a Roman legionnaire doesn't die for Rome in the abstract, but for his fellow Roman legionnaires.

Pontius: Whatever truth he had died with him. That is not a very practical truth and being a practical man is what made me a good governor. Being a practical man allowed me to let the Jews kill a troublemaker and get my problem solved. But as for this dead "king" having held a truth as messiah, well a dead truth is as good as a lie, and I think he is probably a lie as well.

Paul: *(Angry)* Can truth die? Did Jesus die? *His* was the voice I heard after his death. He reprimanded me for persecuting him and his followers. He showed me the truth of his holiness, of my sin, and of the forgiveness he won for me through his death.

Pontius: So, you mean to tell me this troublesome truth continues on from the grave?

Paul: More than that, more than just teachable truth continues; he *himself* lives even though he died, he conquers death, he *is* the way, the truth and the life.

Pontius: This is all very well, inspiring even. But practically speaking, I just don't see the point of it all.

Paul: The point? Jesus Christ conquering death for you? You don't see the point?

Pontius: Let me be blunt: You're here with me in this crummy cell. People still suffer. People still die. You're likely to die very soon. Even if we know the truth, what practical good will it do us now?

Paul: I once wrote to the church here in Rome about this mystery: "As it is written, 'For thy sake we are being killed all the day long; we are regarded as sheep to be slaughtered.' No, in all these things we are more than conquerors ..."

Pointius: Conquerors? How ...

Paul: I'm not through yet ... "We are more than conquerors through him who loved us. For I am sure that neither death, nor life, nor angels, nor principalities, nor things present, nor things to come, nor powers, nor height, nor depth, nor anything else in all creation, will be able to separate us from the love of God in Christ Jesus our Lord."

Pontius: I hear the guards coming. You believe that this is the truth, eh? You better be right.

Paul: My point is, *Jesus* is right. "I am speaking the truth in Christ, I am not lying ..."

Pontius: I wonder which of us will find out first whether or not you live a lie? Which one of us will die first? Will I be first because I misread the truth of the King of the Jews and the *wrong* man was killed? Or will it be you because of your insistence that the *right* man died?

Paul: If you are correct in your doubt, neither of us will ever know. If I'm right — that is, if God is right — and I believe he is — then it's best to be on the side of truth and faith in Christ. Otherwise, you will be in for a sad surprise ...

Pontius: Nothing surprises me more than my actually listening to your gibberish. God's love in a prison cell is a surprise indeed, a lot like the surprise of having the King of the Jews standing next to me while I turn him over to a largely Jewish mob who then kills him. If there's a "truth" that I discovered in this cell tonight, Paul, it's that your impractical God surprises me too much for me to believe in him.

Questions About The Story
Questions For You

(This dialogue is fictional, based on the scripture quotations found in it. However, the basic conflict between God's will and the will of humanity is not fictional. You will be asked questions based on this conflict and see your conflict with God as real because: You're real and God is real.)

1. How did being practical help Pontius in his life?
2. How would being practical help Paul?
3. How would being practical hurt Paul?
4. How does being practical help you in your life?
5. How does it hurt you?
6. What is the "ultimate truth" for you?
7. How do you live this truth?
8. How is God's love in Christ part of your living this truth?

Reflection By A Famous Christian On:
Pragmatism

"Do not deceive yourselves. If you think that you are wise in this age, you should become fools so that you may become wise. For the wisdom of this world is foolishness with God ... For all things are yours — all belong to you and you belong to Christ, and Christ belongs to God.
— Paul from 1 Corinthians 3:18-23 (excerpts)

A Prayer Starter

Dear Christ my Savior, your love does not seem very practical. The wisdom of the world is cynical and selfish and seems successful. The practical truth is that love seems to fail so often in my life, in the nightly news, in history. And, the sad truth is that I don't deserve your love because I have sinned.

But, the happy truth is that you still give me your love because you are my God who is love. Your love is impractical, self-sacrificing and eternal. You send the Holy Spirit to me to lead me in this truth and comfort me with this truth. Guide me to live the truth of God's love in your name. Help me to practice this love.

Suggestions For Practicing Your Prayer

1. God is love. The Holy Spirit is God's breath of life to you. Take a deep breath. Hold it. Think of a fun and impractical act of love for someone before you exhale. Did I surprise you? Take another deep breath of God and try again ...

2. Do you decide to spend time on practical "tasks" or on "relationships?" How do you make this decision?

3. Have you ever considered a "task," a "relationship" or vice versa?

4. How is going to church a "task" for you? Prayer? Tithing? Scripture study? Which do you consider part of a living relationship with God and God's people?

A Suggested Order Of Worship
For
Pontius Pilate, Pragmatic

(Note: You may want to break into small groups for discussion of the story and then join together again for the closing worship. If so, select discussion leaders to help people reflect on the questions in the book. Or, you may want to stay together and reflect silently as the questions are read.)

Opening: Greeting and introduction of "The Conflict Of The Will: Our Doubt Of God Became Flesh Among Us."

Hymns: "What Child Is This" or "Oh Come, Oh Come Emmanuel"

Read: Introduction to Chapter Four, page 41

Reading: Luke 13:1-5; Mark 15:1-15; John 18:28—19:16; 1 Timothy 6:13

Meditation: Pontius Pilate, Pragmatic

Discussion: Break into discussion groups and follow "Questions About The Story/Questions For You" or read aloud for group silent reflection. When finished, quietly return to worship setting.

Read: "Reflections By A Famous Christian"

Read: "Prayer Starter"

Invitation: Invite people to add their own prayers

Read: "Suggestions For Practicing Your Prayer"

The Lord's Prayer

The Apostles' Creed

Hymns: "Take My Life That I May Be" or "Rock Of Ages"

Benediction And Dismissal: "Go in peace and serve the Lord."

chapter five

Judas,
The Obscure

Judas' problem is that he doesn't have any excuse for the thing he does; he has reasons, but no excuses. Have you ever acted in a way you yourself couldn't understand? Dostoyevski noted: "All self-examination ends up as self-justification." But does it?

Concerning Judas' problem: Is he deceiving himself or is he deceiving God?

(Please read Matthew 26:14-25;
Luke 22:3-6; John 6:57-71 and 10:14-18)

Judas

(Judas sits alone in a dark corner.)
This is a confession and I tell you that from the first Judas was an onion of a man. His personality revealed transparent layer-upon-layer, and peeled apart, there was nothing in his center. He had so many motives and excuses for doing what he did that you knew he was making up his life as he lived it.

But did he have to live a lie? Matthew remembers our Lord telling us, "Let your words be, 'Yes, Yes' or 'No, No'; anything more than this comes from the evil one." But Judas was never able to be that direct, never so uncomplicated. Satan had gotten the best of Judas from the beginning and so Judas often devilishly twisted things to mean something they weren't supposed to mean: an evening meal became a setting for betrayal, not communion; a kiss was not a sign of love but a signal for capture.

Judas was doomed because Judas didn't know how to say, "Yes" and mean it or say, "No," and mean no. He was drowning in "maybes," "Could bes," "What ifs." I'll explain this puzzle of Judas ... if I can.

I confess Judas was a puzzle to himself. He was at a loss to know what he himself really felt or thought about anything. How then, not knowing himself, could he have a solid understanding of the Messiah, the Christ, God on earth, our Rabbi, Jesus of Nazareth? At times Judas seemed trustworthy enough. He received the disciples' common purse as treasurer. Perhaps the love of money was the root of his evil? Yet to attribute to 30 pieces of silver this treachery of a pupil to rabbi, creature to creator, man to God is preposterous; God's life should not be had so cheaply.

Why did he betray God-in-the-flesh? I keep wanting to find excuses for him. Maybe Judas was disappointed in Jesus being the eternal God and not a resurrected King David? Maybe Judas sought only to get Jesus out of the way in the confused political situation? Maybe Judas was motivated by his zealous desire for a political overthrow of the Roman occupation? For his betrayal there are so many reasons and no excuses. Brother John remembers Jesus telling us, "... among you there are some who do not believe." As always, Jesus was two steps ahead of us. Maybe that was the reason Judas killed him. Someone once said that if a teacher is only one step ahead of the pupil, the pupil will be fascinated by the teacher's insight. But if the teacher dares to be two steps ahead, the pupil will resent and hate the teacher. The student will seek a way to humiliate the teacher. Maybe Judas felt this way. Jesus called Judas "a devil," and knew from the beginning who was going to betray him. Maybe our Teacher saw the hatred of the false student who would purposely miss the teacher's point out of evil spite.

Yet I know now our Creator Lord never gave up control of the situation — of creation, even though he was betrayed and killed by this creature and his muddled motives. Jesus said, "For this reason the Father loves me, because I lay down my life in order to take it up again. No one takes it from me, but I lay it down of my own accord. I have power to lay it down, and I have power to take it up again. I have received this command from my Father." What would have happened to us all at the death of God?

The death of Judas will change nothing because he is already nothing. Listen to me, for in this, my confession, I defend someone who is not here but has already departed from us. He has no hope except in my despair for him.

Judas reveals himself to be at once a traitor, and at the same time someone who is not able to believe his own duplicity. At the last meal, when Jesus announced, "Truly I tell you, one of you will betray me," Judas had exclaimed at the table, "Surely, not I, Rabbi?" He must have felt like he was watching himself in a nightmare, betraying his Lord and admitting his guilt with his own words of denial. "You have said so," Jesus replied. Judas had betrayed not God but himself.

53

Poor Judas. He removes himself farther and farther from God who is everywhere, from God who is life.

Excuses rush to me for Judas: Judas, separated from hope, from life. Judas was a child of light and yet ran to the darkness. He was a shadow who could only exist because of the light.

It will be said of poor Judas who cannot be excused, of me who makes excuses for Judas, "Let his homestead become desolate, and let there be no one to live in it."

And so it is already true: The homestead to protect me from the dark is open to the dark. Judas is desolate, no one any longer lives in Judas. I no longer live in Judas. I long to die away from my God for I am so ashamed. Yet still could I flee to him; but I will not, for I confess that I cannot bear to see him or myself again.

Questions About The Story
Questions For You

(The soliloquy is fictional, based on the scripture quotations found in it. However, the basic conflict between God's will and the will of humanity is not fictional. The following questions based on this conflict may help you see that your conflict with God is real because: You're real and God is real.)

1. Why do you think Judas betrayed Jesus?
2. After reading the Bible passages, why do you think Judas killed himself? Who is the last "him" in the soliloquy?
3. How could one see Judas as a good man?
4. Could Jesus forgive Judas after all?
5. When did you last betray Jesus' command to love God?
6. When did you last betray Jesus' commandment to love others?
7. When you don't do the "right thing," what is your reason for not doing it? Is that a reason or an excuse?
8. How can keeping your answers limited to "Yes" and "No" help you tell the truth?
9. How can answering only "Yes" and "No" help you to know the truth about yourself and your motives and values?
10. How does the church help you to be honest?
11. How do the sacraments help you to be good?
12. How does society help you to be honest?
13. What sin do you think God could not forgive?
14. Who must you forgive? From whom must you seek forgiveness?

Reflection By A Famous Christian On:
Deceit

"... the words of Cicero so move the heart of everyone, and provoke a sigh: 'There are no snares more dangerous than those which lurk under the guise of duty or the name of relationship. For the man who is your declared foe you can easily baffle by precaution; but the hidden, intestine and domestic danger not merely exists, but overwhelms you before you can foresee and examine it.' "

— St. Augustine in *The City of God*, Book XIX "The Error of Human Judgments" quoting Cicero, *In Verrem* ii. 1. 15

A Prayer Starter

Dear God, you not only speak words but you also speak things. When you say, "Let there be light," then light comes into being. When you love us, you send your only Son to show us your eternal love. Help me through the power of your Word in Christ, to realize the power of words in my life. Help me to be a good steward of words and to say what I mean and mean what I say. Help me to know you better and myself better and serve you and my neighbor honestly and truly.

Suggestions For Practicing Your Prayer

1. Practice saying "Yes" or "No" to questions asked of you.

2. When you say "But" you mean you've lied in what you said before you said "but." Go one day without saying "But . . ."

3. Do you do what you say and say what you do? Find a time each day to examine your words and deeds.

4. Read and memorize 1 John 1:8-9 "If we say we have no sin, we deceive ourselves and the truth is not in us. (Whenever) we confess our sin, he who is faithful and just will forgive our sin and cleanse us from all unrighteousness." Use this as the beginning of your confession each day.

A Suggested Order Of Worship
For
Judas, The Obscure

(Note: You may want to break into small groups for discussion of the story and then join together again for the closing worship. If so, select discussion leaders to help people reflect on the questions in the book. Or, you may want to stay together and reflect silently as the questions are read.)

———————

Opening: Greeting and introduction of "The Conflict Of The Will: Our Violent Opposition To God's Will."

Hymns: "Jesus, Your Blood And Righteousness" or "Just As I Am"

Read: Introduction to Chapter Five, page 51

Reading: Matthew 26:14-25; Luke 22:3-6; John 6:57-71 and 10:14-18

Meditation: Judas, The Obscure

Discussion: Break into discussion groups and follow "Questions About The Story/Questions For You" or read aloud for group silent reflection. When finished, quietly return to worship setting.

Read: "Reflections By A Famous Christian"

Read: "Prayer Starter"

Invitation: Invite people to add their own prayers

Read: "Suggestions For Practicing Your Prayer"

The Lord's Prayer

The Apostles' Creed

Hymns: "Take My Life, That I May Be" or "Rock Of Ages"

Benediction And Dismissal: "Go in peace and serve the Lord."

chapter six

Ananias And Sapphira, Liars

Ananias and Sapphira's problem isn't so much that they had money and didn't give it to the church, but that they lied to God. Remember, money is not the root of all evil; the *love* of money is ...

(Note: Verse 11 contains the first reference to the followers of Christ being called a "church" or ekklesia: *the called out/chosen ones.)*

(Please read Acts 4:32—5:11)

Ananias And Sapphira

Ananias has just been carried out dead. Joseph of Cyprus (the Levite who sold his field and gave the proceeds to the church) and Peter are standing outside the house-church. They watch as the corpse is carried off. A babble of voices is heard from inside the house-church. The church is filled with fear. Peter and Joseph walk away a little to talk.

Joseph: *(Shocked and afraid)* I feel unreal, beside myself. That was awful. Ananias dropped dead. One moment life — the next, death.

Peter: *(Afraid too, but strong; struggling to understand — talking to himself . . .)* One moment the truth, one moment a lie: One moment he was God's child, the next moment he belonged to death.

Joseph: How are we going to tell his wife, Sapphira?

Peter: I imagine that, in a way, she already knows because of her involvement in Ananias' scheme. She'll be around soon to see how things went.

Joseph: Things went badly for Ananias. He just dropped dead. I've never seen anyone so dead so fast.

Peter: He was dead long before he dropped.

Joseph: You mean he was a ghost?

Peter: Scarier than a ghost. He was a living man who lied to God. He was dead the moment he lied because his lying separated him from the truth — and God is truth and life.

Joseph: I remember Jesus telling us, "I am the way, the truth and the life, no one comes to the Father except by me."

Peter: My point exactly, "There is salvation in no one else, for there is no other name under heaven given among mortals by which we must be saved."

Joseph: Didn't mortal Ananias know that though? What got into him? It was like "Satan filled his heart" the way you said.

Peter: Don't overestimate Satan or underestimate our own capacity to sin without his help. Satan, after all, is a bumbler. He foils his own plans because he forgets he is a creature like us — not a creator, not a divinity. There is only one true God. Yet Satan struggles on to deceive the church. He bumbles on showing the church the truth of his lies through his illuminating failures.

Joseph: "Illuminating failures," isn't that what Lucifer means in a way: "The bright one?"

Peter: Hey, that's right. I'd forgotten that old tale: The big pagan fertility god is absent during a drought so a substitute is proposed and the Venus-star, little Lucifer, climbs up into the throne . . .

Joseph: *(Laughing)* . . . But he is too tiny and ridiculous in that big throne and has to climb down again to earth and reign there ashamed and angry. Some god, huh?

Peter: Well, that sounds like our little Lucifer — angry and vengeful, and basically a real loser. Like the Venus Morning Star, he tries to shine in his darkness, but only serves as a doorman for the entrance of the sun. No, Satan is not to be blamed alone for Ananias' lie anyway. Ananias must have planned this on his own pretty well. I asked him, "How is it that you have contrived this in your heart?"

Joseph: He didn't even try to defend himself. He didn't say or do anything.

Peter: Dropping dead is doing something, but I thought he'd at least try to defend himself. I thought his mouth would start opening and closing like the fish we used to catch in Galilee — caught out of their element of life. In fact, he was like a fish caught out of the water. He was suddenly in the realm of the Father of Lies, of death, of separation from our God who is life.

Joseph: I think he realized that and his heart was broken.

Peter: He broke his own heart. He killed himself for money.

Joseph: Was it the money, though? I mean, not all of us have land to sell. I did. So did Ananias. Not many of us have much to give to the church. Did the money kill him?

Peter: There's nothing wrong with having money and land. They're a way to get through life, to care for God's creation, to help others. The *love* of money — that's what kills you. Whether or not you have money, the love of it is the root of all evil — Ananias' evil in this case: the evil of lying to God.

Joseph: So the problem wasn't that he owned land or sold it or even decided to keep some of the money for himself. It's that he contrived to lie about his being part of our communal family of faith. He wanted the money more than the church, more than the truth, more than God.

Peter: That's it. We can't afford to "put the Spirit of the Lord to the test." In short, we can't afford to buy God.

Joseph: Besides, he gives himself freely to us in Jesus.

Peter: Amen to that. I wonder now what Sapphira's end will be?

Joseph: We'll have to confront her with the truth.

Peter: Oh, it can be such a wonderful thing to live in the truth.

Joseph: And such a terrifying life to live if you live a lie.

Peter: There isn't such a thing as a life lived as a lie. It is death plain and simple — as plain as Ananias' death. It's something for us all to remember.

Joseph: Yes, one of those oddly holy lessons that Lucifer assists in teaching us.

Peter: *(Laughing quietly)* I bet you he's mad as a hornet!

Joseph: *(Joining in)* Yes, the Father of Lies foiled again by the truth — who is Christ our Lord.

Questions About The Story
Questions For You

(This playlet is fictional, based on the scripture quotations found in it. However, the basic conflict between God's will and the will of humanity is not fictional. The following questions based on this conflict may help you see that your conflict with God is real because: You're real and God is real.)

1. What were Ananias and Sapphira trying to get away with? Why?
2. When Peter confronts them, does he actually convict them of their act? What actually convicts them?
3. What kills them?
4. How many ways can you think of in which lying kills people?
5. How can the truth "kill" in the midst of lies?
6. How does one learn to lie?
7. How does one learn to tell the truth?
8. How often do you tell the truth? Give a percentage rating.
9. What percentage of "untruth" is left in your life?
10. How can the truth make you free?

Reflection By A Famous Christian On:
Liars

"I write to you, not because you do not know the truth, but because you know it, and you know that no lie comes from the truth. Who is the liar but the one who denies that Jesus is the Christ? No one who denies the Son has the Father; everyone who confesses the Son has the Father also. Let what you heard from the beginning abide in you. If what you heard from the beginning abides in you, then you will abide in the Son and in the Father. And this is what he has promised us, eternal life.''

— 1 John: 2:21, 22a-25

A Prayer Starter

Dear God, it is true that you became flesh and dwelt among us, full of truth and grace in Jesus our Lord. Keep me in this truth and help me to bring others to this truth so that we may live in truth together now and forever.

Suggestions For Practicing Your Prayer

1. Remember the last time you didn't tell the truth. How did you feel? Did the truth finally come out? Did you finally tell the truth? How did it feel then?
2. What truth do you need to tell someone today at work, at home?
3. What truth do you need to admit to yourself?
4. Pick one person to tell the truth to today; one person — one truth.
5. Pick one person to talk to today about Jesus being God.

A Suggested Order Of Worship
For
Ananias And Sapphira, Liars

(Note: You may want to break into small groups for discussion of the story and then join together again for the closing worship. If so, select discussion leaders to help people reflect on the questions in the book. Or, you may want to stay together and reflect silently as the questions are read.)

Opening: Greeting and introduction of "The Conflict Of The Will: Our Trying To Fool God."

Hymns: "We Give Thee But Thine Own" or "God, Our Help In Ages Past"

Read: Introduction to Chapter Six, page 59

Reading: Acts 4:32—5:11

Meditation: Ananias And Sapphira, Liars

Discussion: Break into discussion groups and follow "Questions About The Story/Questions For You" or read aloud for group silent reflection. When finished, quietly return to worship setting.

Read: "Reflections By A Famous Christian"

Read: "Prayer Starter"

Invitation: Invite people to add their own prayers

Read: "Suggestions For Practicing Your Prayer"

The Lord's Prayer

The Apostles' Creed

Hymns: "The Old Rugged Cross" or "Thine Is The Glory"

Benediction And Dismissal: "Go in peace and serve the Lord."